A Hand Up

A HAND UP

Black Philanthropy and Self-Help in America

Emmett D. Carson

JOINT CENTER FOR POLITICAL AND ECONOMIC STUDIES PRESS

The Joint Center ⌐⌐⌐⌐ studies contributes to the national intere⌐⌐⌐ ⌐⌐⌐g black Americans participate fully and effectively in the political and economic life of our society. A nonpartisan, nonprofit institution founded in 1970, the Joint Center uses research and information dissemination to accomplish three objectives: to improve the socioeconomic status of black Americans; to increase their influence in the political and public policy arenas; and to facilitate the building of coalitions across racial lines.

Opinions expressed in Joint Center publications are those of the authors and do not necessarily reflect the views of the other staff, officers, or governors of the Joint Center or of the organizations supporting the Center and its research.

Library of Congress Cataloging-in-Publication Data

Carson, Emmett Davon.
A hand up : Black philanthropy and self-help in America / Emmett D. Carson.
p.   cm.
Includes bibliographical references.
1. Afro-Americans—Charities—History.   2. Afro-Americans—Charitable contributions—History.   3. Philanthropy—History.
I. Joint Center for Political and Economic Studies (U.S.)
II. Title.
HV3181.C38   1992
362.84'96073—dc20   92–28967 CIP

ISBN 1–880285–02–9 (cloth : alk. paper)
ISBN 1–880285–05–3 (pbk. : alk. paper)

© 1993, Joint Center for Political and Economic Studies, Inc.

Joint Center for Political and Economic Studies
1090 Vermont Avenue, N.W., Suite 1100
Washington, D.C. 20005–4961

Contents

Foreword

It has been a widely held belief among Americans, even among many black Americans, that the black community does too little to "help its own," and that if blacks contribute at all to charitable organizations, their contribution represents far less than a "fair share." This perception has taken hold despite ample, if anecdotal, evidence that it is unfounded. As a group of eminent black scholars has pointed out:

> The "self-help" tradition is so embedded in the black heritage as to be virtually synonymous with it. Self-initiated efforts without assistance from the larger society—indeed, often in spite of resistance from the society—have found expression throughout our history in this country. The tradition of building institutions and initiating efforts both to defend themselves and to advance within a hostile society has long been a hallmark of black American life. [1]

In 1986, the Joint Center for Political and Economic Studies undertook the first comprehensive national study of black philanthropy. This research, employing scientific sampling and polling techniques, exploded the myth of black indifference to community needs. The statistical findings of that research were published in 1989 under the title, *The Charitable Appeals Fact Book: How Black and White Americans Respond to Different Types of Fund-Raising Efforts.* Those findings show a clear pattern: Black Americans from every socioeconomic background are widely engaged in charitable activity today, largely through their churches, and this activity goes on at levels equal to or greater than among white Americans. Black Americans today continue to be active participants in a rich philanthropic tradition, giving of their money, goods, time, and expertise to help the needy and to achieve broad objects for the betterment of their community and the society as a whole.

One reason for the relatively low visibility of black philanthropy was uncovered during the research: Blacks donate the majority of their monetary contributions and volunteer hours to black-run or black-serving organizations, and often through their churches. Indeed, thanks to the scope of black churches, established institutions like the NAACP and the United Negro College Fund, and newer groups like the Black United Fund, black Americans have many opportunities to help serve one another directly, without going outside the black community.

Understanding the current vitality of black charitable activity is only one aspect of creating a clearer overall picture of black philanthropy. The caring and generosity that was uncovered through the Joint Center's research is part of a long tradition of giving that reaches back over two centuries of this country's history. This extended essay represents an attempt to sketch out some of the key elements and patterns that give that tradition its unique shape and vitality. As a companion to *The Charitable Appeals Fact Book*, this volume represents an attempt to clarify and round out the picture. Together, these volumes offer the first steps toward correcting public misapprehension about black philanthrophy and self-help today as a traditional reflection of the values of the black community.

It is our hope that the research published earlier, in combination with this historical overview, will both challenge the perception of black dependency in the past, and enhance the effectiveness of black philanthropic initiatives in the future.

We are grateful to Dr. Emmett D. Carson, now program officer at the Ford Foundation, for conducting and coordinating the original research at the Joint Center and for writing this volume. Thanks also to Dr. Milton Morris, vice president for research, who oversaw the project, and to Nancy Stella, communications director, and members of her staff Marc DeFrancis and Tyra Wright, as well as editorial consultants Janet Lowenthal, Laura Baker, and Allison King, all of whom were involved in the book's editing and production.

Eddie N. Williams
President
Joint Center for Political
and Economic Studies

Introduction

There is a rich and deep-rooted history of black philanthropy in this country dating back to colonial days. Humanitarian activity by blacks on behalf of their own communities has been central to their traditions and even their survival for more than two hundred years. Indeed, a number of today's black charitable organizations trace their ancestry back to the colonial period.[2]

The ends pursued by black philanthropic organizations and the means employed to achieve them have much in common with those of these institutions' white counterparts. However, the unique situation of blacks in America has also continued to pose separate issues for black philanthropy and to give it a distinctive character.

The purpose of this extended essay is not to provide a comprehensive chronology of the history of black philanthropy in America; such an undertaking, while clearly worthwhile, is far beyond the scope of this research effort. Rather, the purpose is to discuss some of the key developments, events, and institutions in this rich history, and thus to shed light on the shape and thrust of black philanthropy today through an examination of some of the historical, philosophical, and social forces that have given rise to it.

Defining Forces in Black Philanthropy

As black philanthropic organizations have evolved in response to diverse social, economic and political needs, three overlapping strains or traditions have been present, with varying degrees of emphasis, throughout American history. These strains have defined the goals and formed the paradigm of black philanthropy to the present day:

• humanitarian aid, to ameliorate individual and community hardship when government or personal resources are absent or inadequate;

• self-help, with a particular emphasis on the establishment of black schools and colleges, as well as commercial enterprises such as banks, and insurance companies formed to benefit the community; and

• social change, from the abolition of slavery, to the elimination of all legal, educational, and economic barriers to racial equality.

These broad objectives have been pursued by a combination of institutions rooted in black community life. Since the earliest days of black philanthropy, black churches of all denominations have been at the core of such efforts, and the leadership provided by black ministers is a key element in explaining the profound influence of the black church on the development of black philanthropy. Another reason for the church's preeminent role is that, unlike other black institutions, each church always has had a source of continued financing: its own congregation.[3]

Black Philanthropy and the American Tradition

While black philanthropy owes much of its distinctive character to the particular life conditions of blacks in America, it is, at the same time, part and parcel of the broader philanthropic mainstream of American society, and shares a number of features in common with this tradition, as well. For example, the objectives of humanitarian aid, self-help and social change have been characteristic of white as well as black charitable organizations. The extraordinary emphasis on "voluntarism" within the wider American society undoubtedly influenced the development of black philanthropy, as well. In addition, both white and black philanthropic organizations have championed progressive ideas before these concepts have won the public consensus required for government support. As the Filer Commission's 1975 Report on Philanthropy and Public Needs notes, "charitable groups were in the forefront of ridding society of child labor, abolitionist groups in tearing down the institution of slavery, civic-minded groups in purging the spoils system from public office."[4]

More recently, David Mathews has suggested that philanthropy breeds what he calls "public power" by raising the consciousness of the entire public to a point where major public decision-making is influenced.[5] The abolitionist and the civil rights movements are outstanding examples of this influence, as are the anti-Vietnam War, disarmament and environmental movements.

Often, such movements have notably hastened the decision-making process through innovative direct action—from the lunch counter sit-ins of the late 1950s, to the recent anti-drug neighborhood-watch programs carried out in Washington, D.C., by the Nation of Islam. In short, black as well as white and multi-racial groups have often used their philanthropic resources to promote issues and programs that could not be pursued through established political means or mainstream organizations.

Another feature shared by all U.S. philanthropic organizations is the continual striving to improve fund-raising capabilities, moving from a focus on "charity among friends," to modern fund-raising federations, "charity among strangers." Part four of this essay takes up the subject of some recent innovations in black fundraising.

Philanthropy and the Black Experience

The legal and social obstacles blacks face in America not only created the imperative and set the agenda for black philanthropy; these obstacles have also sharply defined the field in which black philanthropy arose and flourished. Thus black philanthropy has a very pragmatic character. It is shaped both by needs in the black community and limitations imposed by larger forces in the society. Black philanthropy, therefore, emphasizes self-help or self-empowerment, particularly through education; is committed to dismantling obstacles to black progress through political and legal action; and places special value on donations not only of money, but also of time, expertise, and goods. While none of these characteristics is unique to black philanthropy, together they historically have been and remain its hallmark.

Two forces, in particular, that gave rise to black philanthropy are threaded throughout its history to current times. The first is the relationship between black organizations and the government. By definition, the laws banning black associations, legalizing slavery, and therefore requiring black charitable organizations to work in secret, forced such organizations into an adversarial position vis-a-vis the government. The eventual abolition of slavery was only the beginning of decades of struggle to win for blacks the same services, rights and legal status routinely accorded whites. White charitable organizations, by contrast, even when seeking to change government policies or programs, have worked from a vantage point largely within the system.

Second, the role of blacks within American society and, a

related issue, the merits of black separatism, are continuing issues of debate within the black philanthropic tradition, as they are within the larger framework of black social and political thought. The extent to which blacks should try to assimilate into the wider society, or should instead segregate themselves from it, has been a recurring focus of black philanthropic activity, from Marcus Garvey to the Nation of Islam.

The issue persists throughout much of the history of black philanthropy as a series of questions which the black community and its institutions have struggled to answer. What are

---

The legal and social obstacles blacks face in America not only created the imperative and set the agenda for black philanthropy; these obstacles have also sharply defined the field in which black philanthropy arose and flourished.

---

the merits, both in terms of meeting the needs of the black community and of ensuring the continued viability of black philanthropic institutions, of maintaining a separate black philanthropy, with organizations run exclusively by, and serving only, blacks? Conversely, what is the appropriate role of whites within black philanthropic organizations? What, if any role, should white contributors or white staff play in determining the institutional goals and policies of organizations primarily serving the black community?

Early Roots of
Black Philanthropy

Churches' Secular Arm: Benevolent Institutions

The foundations for black philanthropy were laid during the colonial period with the establishment of black churches and, virtually simultaneously, the growth of mutual aid societies and fraternal orders. The relationships among these institutions were close indeed. It was not unusual for black churches to have their own mutual aid societies or fraternal organizations. It was through these benevolent institutions that the churches were able to address the social and material needs of parishioners and the larger community; in that sense, these societies were the secular arm of the church, albeit a separate and independent one, in the black   community.

The Free African Society, founded in Philadelphia in 1786, clearly illustrates the close relationship between black churches and benevolent societies, but in this case, the society actually antedated its affiliated church. The society was established after its founders, Richard Allen and Absalom Jones, were refused the right to pray at a local white church. Their first response was not to form a church of their own (although they later did just that) but, rather, to form a society to provide for the social and economic needs of its members.[6] Under its bylaws, the Free African Society had the obligations:

> ...to hand forth to the needy of This Society, if any should require, the sum of three shillings and nine pence per week of the said money: provided this necessity is not brought on them by their own imprudence.

> ...that the surviving widow of a deceased member should enjoy the benefit of this society so long as she remains his widow, complying with the rules thereof, excepting the suscriptions [sic].

> ...that the children of our deceased member be under the care of the Society, so far as to pay for the education of their children, if they cannot attend the free school; also to put them out apprentices to suitable tasks or places if required.[7]

By 1788 the Free African Society was receiving daily applications for membership, and its underlying concept— "free and autonomous worship in the Afro-American tradition, and the solidarity and social welfare of the black community"—spread rapidly to other cities.[8] These societies were churches in every sense of the term, save the denominational label. Their membership qualifications read like a list of Christian virtues, including sobriety, fidelity within marriage, and abstinence from a host of "worldly pleasures."[9]

The society also aided the larger community in times of

8

crisis. During the great plague that struck Philadelphia in 1793, it provided the city with an extensive array of voluntary aid including nursing and burial services. In addition, the society was active in the abolitionist movement. [10]

Boston's Sons of the African Society came into being two years after Allen and Jones created their society in Philadelphia. Founded to provide burial services for its members and assistance to widows and children, the Boston Society quickly became an important local institution. The society was so

Black clergymen were often the most educated and dynamic people in their communities, and they frequently transformed their congregations into political organizations that addressed social, political, and economic issues.

widely recognized for community service and charitable activities that in 1808 two hundred blacks attended a commemoration program in its honor.[11]

The fraternal orders and other mutual aid organizations represented much of the collective black leadership of the 1700s and 1800s, and were often directed by or founded with the blessing of the black church. Black clergymen were often the most educated and dynamic people in their communities, and they frequently transformed their congregations into political organizations that addressed social, political, and economic issues.

Allen and Jones actually reversed the order, illustrating the close historic ties between black churches and self-help. In 1787, one year after launching the Free African Society together, each of the men founded a black church: the Bethel African Methodist Episcopal Church and the St. Thomas Protestant Episcopal Church, respectively. These were among the first black churches in the United States. Allen's church led to the creation of a new denomination, African Methodist Episcopal (A.M.E.), in 1816. The African Methodist Episcopal Zion denomination was established in 1820, also, in part, because of segregation. Thus, the church-based activism that came to full flower in the civil rights movement of the 1960s is firmly rooted in over two centuries of black tradition.

Meeting Distinctive Black Needs

The earliest benevolent institutions were formed by black freedmen, the small number of blacks who were not slaves but who were nevertheless forced to live a second-class existence, denied the most basic rights expressed by the Declaration of Independence and guaranteed by the nation's newly-adopted Constitution. As Robert Harris states:

> ... the early black benevolent societies as voluntary associations were not mirror-images or exaggerated forms of similar white organizations. They grew simultaneously with white voluntary associations. Moreover, they served different functions because of the distinctive needs of the free black populace, many of whom had recently emerged from slavery. Common historical experiences, shared African ancestry, cultural affinities, and similar grievances brought free Blacks together into benevolent societies to provide a sense of security in their new status as freemen. [12]

Mutual aid societies, as their name implies, provided their members with a variety of services, including sick dues, burial insurance, and, occasionally, support for a deceased member's widow and children. Fraternal organizations, on the other hand, were limited to men, and were created primarily for fellowship. Generally, all three kinds of organizations restricted membership according to status, income, or gender, and most required their members to lead "moral lives," in some instances expelling members for such improprieties as drunkenness, indebtedness, and extramarital affairs.

Some organizations even used color as an eligibility requirement. The Brown Fellowship Society, founded in 1790 in Charleston, South Carolina, admitted only lighter-complexioned blacks, that is, mulattoes. Given that mulattoes at the time were commonly perceived by the white population as more socially acceptable, it is likely that they held better jobs as freedmen than their darker-hued cousins and, therefore, were more likely to have the income and status that were required to join many of the benevolent and fraternal groups.

One measure of the value that churches, mutual aid societies, and fraternal organizations held for blacks in offering leadership and services and as focal points for changing the circumstances of blacks' lives is the white society's efforts to eliminate them. By 1723 Maryland had established laws restricting independent religious meetings by blacks. This situation did not change after the nation won its independence from Britain. By 1835, several states, including Virginia, Maryland, and North Carolina, had established laws banning fraternal organizations and mutual aid societies outright. Specifically, blacks were prohibited from forming "lyceums, lodges, fire companies, or literary, dramatic, social, moral, or charitable societies."[13] These laws required many black organizations to operate in secret, particularly in the South.

Blacks developed mutual aid societies, however, not only because they were banned from joining similar white organizations, but to meet their own communal needs. Some of the impetus that led free blacks to create their own mutual aid societies can be traced back to Africa, where secret societies were commonly formed for the mutual benefit of members.[14]

Mutual Aid Societies and Fraternal Orders

One of the earliest black mutual aid societies on record was the fraternal society known as African Lodge No. 459, founded by Prince Hall.[15] The lodge, which had chapters in several states, received its formal charter from the Grand Lodge of England in 1787. It had been operating for several years before that charter, and is widely recognized as the first black freemasons' society in the United States. The lodge provided its members not just with social recreation, but, more important, with protection against the possibility of enslavement for delinquent debts.[16] It participated in the abolitionist movement and sponsored regular programs to aid the poor, including collecting and distributing free food and firewood during the winter.

Comprehensive information about the development of these societies during this early era is nonexistent; what evidence there is, however, suggests that the number of mutual aid organizations was growing and that they were financially strong. For example, between 1813 and 1838, the number of these societies in Philadelphia increased from 11 to 100. By 1838, the organizations in Philadelphia had a collective membership of 7,448, total revenues of $18,851, and overall expenditures of $14,172. By 1848, 76 of the 106 mutual aid organizations in Philadelphia had a combined total income of $16,814.23 and had assisted 681 families, paying sick benefits of one and a half to three dollars weekly and death benefits of $10 to $20. [17]

These organizations were also noted for their efforts to reduce crime and help the poor. According to Robert Harris, the success of Philadelphia's black charitable organizations was such that "free blacks required public charity at a rate lower than their proportion of the city's inhabitants."[18]

Several other mutual aid societies, as well as a number of fraternal organizations, operated on a national level with chapters in several states. These include the Grand United Order of Odd Fellows, formed in 1787, which was probably the largest secret organization during this period; the Independent Order of Good Samaritans, founded in 1847; the International Order of Twelve Knights; and the Daughters of Tabor. These latter two, both founded in 1855, were active antislavery societies.

Self-Help Through Education

Black benevolent associations participated actively in meeting community social needs. Like the black churches, they provided the poor not only with basic necessities but with free or subsidized education, and they gave the black community as a whole the financial resources and willing workers needed to help promote self-improvement and challenge social injustices. In effect, they were community foundations.[19]

Education was a special concern of many churches and mutual aid organizations. The Brown Fellowship Society provided education for free black children. The African Benevolent Society, established in Newport, Rhode Island, operated and financed a free school for children of all colors. Members were required to pay an initiation fee of 50 cents. Similarly, the New York African Society for Mutual Relief, founded in 1808, bought a building and established New York City's first black grammar school.[20]

Black literary societies, such as the Philadelphia Library Company of Colored Persons and Baltimore's Young Men's Mental Improvement Society for the Discussion of Moral and Philosophical Questions of All Kinds, became increasingly

13

widespread by the beginning of the nineteenth century, making books and libraries available to the black reader.[21]

Philanthropy for Social Change: the Underground Railroad

Self-help and self-improvement alone were not sufficient to transform the lot of black Americans. Social customs, laws, and institutions had to be changed if true justice was to be achieved. The U.S. Census recorded that in 1860, just before the outbreak of the Civil War, more than 90 percent of the four million blacks then living in the Southern states were slaves. The fact of slavery and the response of blacks and whites to it defined a new direction for black philanthropy: social change.

The movement known as the Underground Railroad can be viewed as the first major effort of black philanthropy dedicated to bringing about social change.

The movement known as the Underground Railroad can be viewed as a nationwide philanthropic effort by black and white opponents of slavery to free the slaves—and as the first major effort of black philanthropy dedicated to bringing about social change. Initiated around 1804 and operating until the outbreak of the Civil War, the movement helped slaves to escape from the South and then to cope with the hostile society they met elsewhere. The Underground Railroad carried out national and international fund-raising campaigns, and black business people were among those who regularly contributed time and money.[22]

The membership of the Underground Railroad was interracial. Both blacks and whites served voluntarily as agents or "conductors" on this railroad of escape, and offered their homes as stations. They not only transported and protected the fugitive slaves, but fed, clothed and sheltered them, and occasionally gave them money with which to make their way. Historian Larry Gara's account of William Still, a black conductor for the Philadelphia vigilance committee, illustrates the leadership role blacks played in this movement:

> Two of the forgotten characters in the popular legend [the Underground Railroad] are the Negro members of various vigilance committees and the fugitives themselves. If it required strong character to be an abolitionist, it took even more courage to become a hunted fugitive or one of his colored abettors....
>
> One of the principal activities of the new Philadelphia vigilance committee was to extend financial aid to fugitives. The committee provided money to board fugitives with families of free Negroes, sometimes for as long as thirteen days but usually for only a few days....The committee also purchased clothing, medicine, and the fugitives' railroad fares to Canada. It advertised anti-slavery meetings in the newspapers and on one occasion spent twenty dollars for handbills and other expenses of a meeting. [23]

It is believed that 100,000 slaves escaped between 1810 and 1850, many using the Underground Railroad. This was accomplished through the combined efforts of a large number of mutual aid societies and vigilance committees, as the individual groups supporting the Railroad were called. One such group, the Knights of Liberty, founded by the Reverend Moses Dickson, had 50,000 members in 1856.[24]

Mutual aid societies assisted the North in the overall war effort, providing volunteer nurses and raising money for families whose men had gone off to battle. They also helped teach newly freed slaves how to read and write.

The Expansion of Black Benevolent Organizations and Schools

After the Civil War, blacks hoped for a better position in American life and, indeed, during the first post-war decade they did make important social, political, and economic gains. However, these gains were short-lived. After its presidential victory in 1876, the Republican party, under mounting pressure from Democrats in the South, abandoned all attempts to protect the rights of blacks. To avoid the possibility of a second civil war, President Rutherford B. Hayes made several political concessions to the South. One of these, "the Hayes-Tilden compromise," gave Southern states "the right to control their own affairs in their own way," that is, the license to handle race relations however their governments chose.[25]

The Hayes-Tilden compromise had important consequences for the evolution of black philanthropy. For blacks it meant a return to second-class citizenship, a status they were determined to fight through racial solidarity and education. As historian August Meier states:

> ...it was clear that the main themes in Negro thinking on the race problem were that for the most part Negroes must work out their own salvation in a hostile environment and that furthermore, they must be united in their efforts at racial elevation.[26]

In the wake of the Hayes-Tilden compromise, the number of mutual aid societies increased substantially. By this time, almost every black church in the country had one or more such societies attached to it.[27] The Odd Fellows burgeoned after the Civil War. It is reported to have had 89 lodges and 4,000 members in 1868; 1,000 lodges and 36,858 members by 1886; 2,047 lodges and 155,537 members by 1896; and, over 4,000 lodges and almost 300,000 members by 1904.[28]

Blacks realized they would have to be united to ensure their own social and economic survival and to advance themselves. Like the mutual aid societies formed before the Civil War, many of the new ones were formed by church

For blacks the Hayes-Tilden compromise meant a return to second-class citizenship, a status they were determined to fight through racial solidarity and education.

leaders concerned with the basic needs of their parishioners, which extended even to their funeral costs. In Philadelphia, for example, the Crucifixion Church led to the establishment of the Crucifixion Society, and the Wesley A.M.E. Church was affiliated with the Avery Society.[29]

Black churches also played a direct, major role in the drive to increase the educational attainment of blacks, establishing a large number of elementary schools, high schools, and colleges. Between 1800 and 1900, the A.M.E. church alone allocated over one million dollars to help maintain the 20 colleges and universities it had founded. In 1908, the American Baptist Home Missionary Society established 23 black institutions of higher education, 14 of them owned by blacks. And for the 5,000 schools constructed for blacks by the white philanthropist Julius Rosenwald, the black community, primarily through the church, contributed 17 percent of the total cost.[30]

The Black Women's Club Movement

Membership in many of the early mutual aid societies was restricted to men. Women had always been active within the church, however, and began to form their own organizations well before Emancipation.[31]

One of the first such organizations was Boston's African-American Female Intelligence Society, established in 1832. In addition to providing its members with health insurance and other services, the society sponsored forums and lectures for the general public. Other early Bostonian organizations that provided community service were the Daughters of Zion, founded in 1845, and the Female Benevolent Firm, founded in 1850.[32] The latter group also sponsored educational programs.

Black women's organizations have participated in a wide range of philanthropic causes. The Daughters of Tabor, founded in 1855, was an antislavery society. The Women's Loyal Union was founded in 1892 to help combat lynching. The White Rose Industrial Association, established in New York in 1898, helped young black women migrating from the South find jobs and provided them with a place to live so they would not be lured into prostitution. The White Rose organization also offered cultural programs, recreational activities, and classes in black history. All these services were provided to thousands of women, often at no charge.[33]

The formation of black women's organizations really gained ground during the last decade of the 19th century, with the establishment of associations far too numerous to list here. Their development, referred to collectively as the black women's club movement, occurred primarily for two reasons.[34] First, many of the organizations evolved out of black women's concern for the welfare of their children in a segregated society. Second, these women had come to resent being characterized as "ignorant and immoral" by the larger society, and being barred on that basis from participating even in suffrage organizations of progressive white women.

The major concerns of black women at this time were eloquently expressed by Josephine St. Pierre Ruffin in her keynote address at the first national convention of black women, held in Boston on July 29-31, 1895:

> The reasons why we should confer are so apparent that it would seem hardly necessary to enumerate them, and yet there are none of them but demand our serious consideration. In the first place we need to feel the cheer and inspiration of meeting each other....
> Next, we need to talk over those things that are of special interest to us as colored women, the training of our children, openings for our boys and girls, how they can be prepared for occupations and occupations may be found that are open for them, what we especially can do in moral education and physical development, the home training that is necessary to give our children in order to prepare them to meet the peculiar conditions in which they shall find themselves, how to make the most of our own, to some extent, limited opportunities....
>
> I have left the strongest reason for our conferring together until the last. All over America there is to be found a large and growing class of earnest, intelligent, progressive colored women who, if not leading full, useful lives, are only waiting for the opportunity to do so, many of them still warped and cramped for lack of opportunity, not only to do more, but to be more; and yet, if an estimate for the colored woman is called for, the inevitable reply, glibly given, is: "For the most part, ignorant and immoral, some exceptions of course, but these don't count."[35]

19

The strongest reason for black women to organize separately, according to Ruffin, was to refute the negative images of black women then being advanced by many in the women's suffrage movement, which at the time often refused to admit black women as members. These white suffragists were afraid of losing white financial support if they allowed black

The strongest reason for black women to organize separately was to refute the negative images of black women then being advanced by many in the women's suffrage movement. . .

women to participate.[36] Ruffin also emphasized the special concern of black women for the future of their children—a principal reason black women have been so active in black philanthropy throughout history.

By 1896, black women had launched the National Association of Colored Women, dedicated to social welfare activities. Its motto was "Lifting as We Climb." During this period, various chapters of the organization aided the homeless and maintained employment services, day care centers, and kindergartens. Black women's clubs were, on the whole, a powerful force in charity directed toward the black community.

* * *

A noteworthy aspect of black charitable institutions since the beginning has been their comprehensive nature. Almost all black organizations had to serve a multiplicity of purposes in the earliest days, in response to the conditions of black life. For example, black churches have always provided spiritual, moral, and political leadership, as well as services for the needy. By the same token, black social and fraternal organizations have long provided social services to the black community, even though their primary mission is to offer fellowship and professional networking for their own members. This heritage remains embedded in these organizations and their offspring to the present day.

The Modern Era
Black Advocacy Comes of Age

Debate on Directions: Washington vs. Du Bois

At the beginning of the twentieth century two extraordinary black leaders emerged: Booker T. Washington and William Edward Burghardt (W.E.B.) Du Bois. These two men led opposite poles of the debate on black progress, and diverged radically in the strategies they recommended for achieving racial equality. The views expressed in this debate each reflected schools of thought that continue to exist today within black philanthropy and institutions.

Booker T. Washington, an ex-slave and founder of the Tuskegee Institute, urged blacks to focus on self-improvement and vocational training as the primary avenues for social and economic advancement. Numerous black organizations formed to put this self-improvement philosophy into practice. The Farmers' Improvement Society of Texas, for example, was founded in 1890 to assist rural blacks with housing, provide health and life insurance, and encourage blacks to extricate themselves from sharecropping. By 1909, the society numbered 21,000 members, had opened offices in Oklahoma and Arkansas, and had established an agricultural college and a black bank. Another of the organizations created to fulfill Washington's vision was the Afro-American League, also founded in 1890, which stressed racial solidarity and business development as the fundamental tools for achieving racial equality. The league remained active for 20 years.[37]

In marked contrast to Washington, Du Bois, a Harvard Ph.D., believed that the growing number of educated blacks, whom he dubbed "the talented tenth," should wage a direct assault on the segregation and peonage blacks then faced, including their nearly total disenfranchisement from the political process. His views were no less influential than Washington's in shaping black thinking of the period. In words that are as meaningful today as they were in 1916, Du Bois highlighted the potential of philanthropy to advance the rights and standing of black Americans:

> We [blacks] must avoid, in the advancement of the Negro race, the mistakes of ruthless exploitation which have marked modern economic history. To this end, we must seek not simply home ownership, small landholding and saving accounts, but also all forms of cooperation, both in production and distribution, profit sharing, building and loan associations, systematic charity for definite, practical ends, systematic migration from mob rule and robbery to freedom and enfranchisement, the emancipation of women and the abolition of child labor. [38]

Du Bois concluded his statement by stressing philanthropy's importance and reiterating the broad definition of purpose that shaped black philanthropy from its earliest days:

For the accomplishments of all these ends we must organize. . . . Organization is sacrifice. It is sacrifice of opinions, of time, of work and of money, but it is, after all, the cheapest way of buying the most priceless of gifts—freedom and efficiency.[39]

Black Fraternities and Sororities

Flowing directly out of Du Bois' philosophy came black fraternities and sororities. Indeed, the Greek letter societies blacks formed during the early 1900s, with their strong tradition of voluntarism and charitable giving, can be considered the "talented tenth's" response to Du Bois' call. As one of the founders of Alpha Phi Alpha, the first black college fraternity, stated:

> ... we wanted more than the traditional American college fraternity. Our job ahead required a fellowship which would embrace those millions outside the "talented tenth." We realized that the leaders of any people emerge chiefly from the best trained, best oriented members of the group.[40]

Between 1906 and 1924, eight black fraternities and sororities were founded: Alpha Phi Alpha (1906), Alpha Kappa Alpha (1908), Omega Psi Phi (1911), Phi Beta Sigma (1914), Kappa Alpha Psi (1911), Delta Sigma Theta (1913)[41], Zeta Phi Beta (1920), and Sigma Gamma Rho (1922). These societies continue today to be active in philanthropy, sponsoring programs to mentor disadvantaged youths, for example, and raising money for scores of charitable endeavors.

New Challenges on the Home Front

The end of the First World War in 1918, like the end of the

Civil War, was a turning point for black Americans. As before, blacks believed that in fighting faithfully for their country they had earned the chance to improve their lot in American society. And just as before, their hopes were dashed. Black soldiers returning home after World War I were often greeted with physical violence, particularly in the South. During the "Red Summer" of 1919, 26 race riots erupted across the country, enveloping Northern as well as Southern cities.

The fuse that lit a good portion of the postwar urban rioting had two strands: black migration and the insecurity of white ethnic workers.

The federal government, under President Woodrow Wilson, was no more interested than the states had been at the close of the Civil War in fostering racial equity. Wilson ignored repeated appeals from black leaders and refused to halt the growing segregation of federal workers at offices and other worksites in the nation's capital.[42]

The fuse that lit a good portion of the postwar urban rioting had two strands: black migration, and the insecurity of white ethnic workers. Southern blacks had begun moving en masse to the Northern cities shortly before World War I, drawn by manufacturing jobs. The influx accelerated after the war, creating two pressing problems.

First, the demand for jobs and adequate housing among these new urban blacks came to far outweigh the supply. Second, the increasing concentration of blacks in the North exacerbated racial tensions, especially between blacks and recent white working-class immigrants, who feared for their new-found status and economic security.

These conditions, coupled with violence, injustice, and government indifference, led to massive and widespread frustration among blacks. Out of this frustration emerged a new type of philanthropic institution, one designed to meet the needs of an expanding and increasingly sophisticated black population determined to achieve equality. This new thrust defined the direction for two young organizations, both founded between 1909 and 1910: the National League on Urban Conditions, later to become the Urban League, and the National Association for the Advancement of Colored People.

The Urban League was founded as a multiracial organization whose purpose was to aid urban blacks through community-based chapters. The league's early activities included helping blacks who had migrated North to find adequate jobs and housing, as well as sponsoring recreational activities to deter delinquency and crime.[43]

The National Association for the Advancement of Colored People (NAACP) had as its stated objective "to make 11,000,000 [black] Americans physically free from peonage, mentally free from ignorance, politically free from disfranchisement, and socially free from insult."[44]

From today's perspective, "peonage" and "insult" seem mere euphemisms for the brutal realities that the NAACP sought to combat. Racial violence against black citizens, including widespread lynchings, reached its worst excesses during this period.[45] The NAACP was very active in response to the crime of lynching. Among its other protests, the group organized an anti-lynching march of 100,000 people in New York, in 1917.[46]

Du Bois, one of the NAACP's founders, voiced considerable satisfaction that the organization was well funded by black philanthropists:

> I thank God that most of the money that supports
> the National Association for the Advancement of
> Colored People comes from black hands; a still
> larger proportion must so come, and we must not

> only support but control this and similar organizations and hold them unwaveringly to our objects, our aims and our ideals.[47]

With the exception of Du Bois, however, all of the first officers of the organization were white, a feature that would continue to cause considerable dissension and debate within the NAACP in particular and among black philanthropic organizations more generally. The question of whether blacks could or should "go it alone" or should embrace white support had long been a concern within black institutions.

The key issue in this ongoing debate has been whether with white contributions came white control. Throughout the country during the late 1800s to early 1900s, for example, blacks had made efforts to limit white control of their institutions. In Atlanta, for example, a group of black Baptists withdrew their support from the Atlanta Baptist College over the issue of racial control, in an unsuccessful attempt to form their own independent school.[48] Concerning the effect of white philanthropy on the black community during this period, scholar King Davis notes that black needs became blurred, and that this obscurity affected the whole future development of black philanthropy: [49]

> With the entry of White financial support came differing definitions of black problems and a perceptible shift in the priorities, tactics, and timetable employed to bring about social change....Although it was not realized at the time, the events of the 1800s formulated the basis for the conflict between whites and blacks in the field of philanthropy and social service.[50]

Assimilation or Separatism: Du Bois vs. Garvey

The debate over the proper relationship of black self-help and philanthropy to the larger white society became a prominent feature of the debate that grew up in the years following World War I around two central figures. Just as Booker T. Washington and W.E.B. Du Bois had shaped the discussion of race relations in the years before the war, so Du Bois and Marcus Garvey, a Jamaican immigrant, shaped them after.

In 1914, Garvey founded the Universal Negro Improvement Association (UNIA). The aim of UNIA, which functioned as a mutual aid society, was to promote racial pride among blacks. Members paid dues in order to receive sickness and burial insurance. The society publicized a number of familiar philanthropic goals, among them: administering and assisting the needy; establishing universities, colleges, and secondary schools for blacks; and "civilizing the backward tribes of Africa."[51]

However, some of Garvey's views were far more controversial. One of his central arguments was that blacks should limit assistance from whites, and completely control and operate their own businesses and institutions. Garvey took Du Bois' advocacy for black support and control of black organizations one step further: he argued that blacks would never achieve true social justice in America, and therefore advocated that they emigrate to Africa.

Du Bois, on the other hand, continued to advocate protest, but only within the legal limits of democracy. He also favored interracial cooperation. The bitter debate between Du Bois and Garvey, pitting more established views on charity and social reform against a radical approach to black independence, would have a continuing impact on black philanthropy. Three fundamental questions emerged from this debate: Did Du Bois' talented tenth adequately represent the aspirations of most blacks? What role should whites play in black organizations? And finally, should blacks remain in the United States, or seek an alternative destiny in Africa?

Garvey had the support of hundreds of thousands of blacks. Even his staunchest critics recognized that he had succeeded in reviving blacks' faith in their own abilities and self-worth. Garvey's success may be partly attributable to his

---

When the stock market crashed on October 29, 1929, plunging the United States into the Great Depression, blacks were hit particularly hard as newly unemployed whites began to compete for their jobs.

---

clear understanding of the depth of blacks' frustration over their social and economic conditions, and the inability of established black leaders to achieve rapid changes.[52]

The debate Garvey started ended abruptly in 1927 when the U.S. government deported him for alleged tax evasion. UNIA, too, was dissolved after many leaders in the black establishment sent a letter to the U.S. attorney general, asking him to "completely disband and extirpate this vicious movement."[53] (Du Bois, to his credit, did not sign the letter.)

This move by leading blacks to discredit Garvey may have justified Garvey's earlier pronouncement that "the Negro is his own greatest enemy."[54] In any case, the destruction of Garvey's public efforts put to rest, at least temporarily, two of the issues. First, there would be no back to Africa movement for blacks. Second, blacks would continue to accept the help of whites in the effort to secure the rights of full citizenship.

Humanitarian Aid During the Great Depression

The new thrust of black philanthropy toward changing the social conditions of blacks in this country augmented but did not replace the self-help and mutual aid begun by the earliest societies. When the stock market crashed on October 29, 1929, plunging the United States into the Great Depression, blacks were hit particularly hard as newly unemployed whites began to compete for their jobs.[55] Although President Franklin Roosevelt's New Deal programs were very helpful to blacks during this period, they were not adequate to the enormous need. Blacks therefore resorted to a multitude of modest philanthropic efforts for mutual support. In the North, they organized parties to help neighbors raise money for food and rent. Local storefront churches provided the needy with food and shelter.

One well-known undertaking during this time was the "Peace Mission" in New York's Harlem, operated by Major ("Father") Morgan J. Divine. Divine operated grocery stores nationwide, fed the hungry full meals for 10 cents apiece at his own restaurants, and published and distributed newspapers and magazines for which his followers often volunteered to work. He was also known for the free meals he provided the hungry on Sundays.[56]

A. Philip Randolph and the Fight Against Segregation

Improving the lives of blacks, the overriding goal of black philanthropy, came to be seen, more and more, as inextricably linked with efforts to end segregation. In 1941, as the nation entered the Second World War, black Americans openly debated the wisdom of fighting for a country that still refused to treat them as equals. Segregation in the defense industry, in particular, was loudly denounced by the NAACP, the National Urban League, and scores of black churches, fraternities, sororities, and other groups.

The issue culminated that same year when Asa Philip Randolph, against the advice of many white supporters, led the NAACP, the Urban League, and Randolph's own union, the Brotherhood of Sleeping Car Porters, in delivering an ultimatum to President Roosevelt: Unless the President issued an executive order forbidding discrimination in the

---

In preparing to march on Washington, Randolph was marching figuratively, as well, in the mainstream tradition of black self-help.

---

defense industry and the federal government, Randolph would lead a march of 100,000 blacks on Washington. Roosevelt responded by issuing Executive Order 8802, thereby averting the march. This effort on the part of blacks represented the strongest federal civil rights action since Reconstruction.[57]

It is especially significant that Randolph's group was able to win a major victory for civil rights by threatening a march consisting exclusively of black volunteers. In preparing to march on Washington, Randolph was marching figuratively, as well, in the mainstream tradition of black self-help, as his summing up of the rationale for the march illustrates:

> The essential value of an all-Negro movement such as the [planned] March on Washington is that it helps to create faith by Negroes in Negroes. It develops a sense of self-reliance, with Negroes depending on Negroes in vital matters. It helps to break down the slave psychology and inferiority-complex in Negroes which comes and is nourished with Negroes relying on white people for direction and support.

Randolph went on to comment on the voluntary nature of the march, in words with relevance for the discussions that continue to this day over whether blacks should nurture separate charitable organizations of their own:

> As a rule, Negroes do not choose to be [i.e., to keep] to themselves in anything; they are only to themselves as a result of compulsive segregation. Negroes are together voluntarily for the same reason workers join voluntarily into a trade union. But because workers . . . join trade unions does not mean that the very same workers may not join organizations composed of some nonworkers, such as art museums or churches or fraternal lodges, that have varying purposes. The same thing is true of Negroes.[58]

Philanthropy Today
Building for the Future

The strategies that brought the sweeping social changes of the civil rights era represented not so much a new direction as a shifting of emphasis. During the 1940s, A. Philip Randolph had waged a direct assault on government policies that winked at segregation in the federal workplace and defense industries, using the power of threatened protest to apply pressure to the Executive branch of government. During the 1950s and '60s, activists continued to use protest for leverage, taking to the streets to press Congress to meet their demands for justice. At the same time, the NAACP made the case against segregation in the courts. The NAACP's successful challenge to segregation in the public schools, *Brown v. Board of Education*, was the culmination of a concerted black philanthropic effort to win fundamental social change.

The institutions, the strategies, and the philanthropic activity that characterized the civil rights era and that fueled great transformations in American life are directly descended from the activities and institutions of the previous two centuries. The emphasis on education and voluntarism, of giving time and talents for the "cause," and on pushing for systemic change are themes inherent throughout the history of black philanthropy. Between 1957 and 1968, black organizations directed the efforts of tens of thousands of people, mostly blacks, in a national civil rights protest movement whose principal features were familiar: raising money, collecting and distributing food, and carefully orchestrating boycotts, sit-ins, and marches. The civil rights movement of the 1960s presents, in microcosm, the main features of black self-help and philanthropy throughout history.

Role of the Church. The black church stood at the forefront of this movement, just as it had in the development of mutual aid societies and in the abolitionist movement. As one of the most widely respected black institutions and the one with the largest membership, it held the power to galvanize black Americans from all socioeconomic classes and summon them to action.

Volunteering for Action. The eventual success of countless demonstrations for civil rights was due largely to the voluntary participants, including children, who were the movement's heart and substance. Like their predecessors in the Underground Railroad of a century before, these volunteers contributed materially and spiritually to the effort—and at considerable personal risk. They demonstrated, themselves, and they fed and sheltered other demonstrators in their homes. They were often harassed and beaten, and many lost their lives. Sadly, white resistance to their cause was to be found even among philanthropic groups. In several Southern communities, for instance, black organizations such as the Urban League lost substantial funding because they were denied local community chest support.[59]

Marching as One. The power of organizing and of marching to move public policy, revealed before World War II by A. Philip Randolph, became a central element. In 1963, taking a page from Randolph, more than 200,000 people representing over 400 organizations marched on Washington, where Martin Luther King riveted the nation with his "I Have A Dream" speech calling for a new national vision of a colorblind society.[60] Through this march, it is widely believed, the civil rights movement prevailed on Congress to pass the Civil Rights Act of 1964. Similarly, the passage of the Voting Rights Act of 1965 is widely attributed to another march, the one from Selma to Montgomery in 1965. The marchers had learned to pressure the system to reform itself.

Revived Support for Black Separatism. The debate over black separatism that Marcus Garvey led until his deportation in 1927 was reprised during the civil rights era, as well. In the aftermath of the assassinations of Martin Luther King, Jr., and Robert Kennedy, the sentiment for armed conflict grew among some members of the black community. Many blacks became drawn to the Nation of Islam, led by its chief spokesman Malcolm X, and Elijah Muhammad, the movement's leader until his death in 1975. Although the Nation of Islam had been established in 1930, its black nationalist orientation found its most receptive audience in the 1960s among black youth who were vocal in demanding immediate economic equality by any means necessary. Indeed, there are striking parallels between this movement and the earlier separatist movement led by Marcus Garvey. While some observers find the Nation of Islam's separatist ideology and militant style somewhat extreme, the organization's volunteer services have been widely credited for their work in rehabilitating criminals, alcoholics, and drug addicts. [61]

While some blacks were responsive to the Nation of Islam's appeal, most remained sympathetic throughout the civil rights era to King's dream of a colorblind, integrated society achieved through peaceful means. And throughout the late 1960s, years following that speech, many legal barriers to equality and integration were overthrown. Nevertheless, as the nation entered the 1970s, the issue of separatism would continue to arise—in the philanthropic arena as elsewhere, as blacks questioned whether they should engage in philanthropic activity independently or in concert with whites.

The Power of the Pulpit

The philanthropic leadership and resources of the black church have proven pivotal throughout the history of black advancement, and they continue to be decisive in the day-to-day life of the black community today.

Black churches are still the most active organizations, by far, when it comes to supporting black charitable activities.[62] These activities can be divided into three broad categories: money raised by the church for other organizations; services provided by the church itself and supported by church donations and volunteers; and services provided by the church but supported with funds from government and foundations.

Today, as in the past, the black churches are a source of political leadership and leaders.

The relationships between black churches and government have become extensive and complex, with the churches frequently offering community services in cooperation with government agencies. This may mean distributing food in government programs; participating in counseling, referral, and social service networks; and actually receiving public funds to operate Headstart, day care, and summer youth programs. Such funding relationships with public bodies tend to be particularly strong in the cities such as New Orleans, Detroit, Atlanta, and Washington, D.C., that are governed by black mayors.

The close relationship between black churches and black elected officials has historic roots. In 1889, a statement by Philip A. Bruce described the close link between church and political action:

> The preachers of the negroes are their most active politicians, as a rule, but even when they are not they have much political influence, for they constitute, individually, the natural leaders of their race, being elevated to their clerical position not because they are men of greater holiness of life or eloquence of tongue than the rest of their fellows, but because they have more energy and decision of character. Each one brings these qualifications to bear on all occasions of public agitation from the conspicuous coigne of vantage, his pulpit, which thus becomes a rostrum, the religious doctrines enunciated from thence taking the color of his political principles, just as, on the other hand, his political harangues have a religious echo. The two parts of minister and orator are played so skillfully at one and the same time that it is impossible to distinguish them; and the affairs of the Hereafter and a contemporary political canvass are mixed in inextricable confusion. His church is thus converted into a political organization that is consolidated by the religious fervor that pervades it, and propelled towards a single political end by a religious enthusiasm that expects to be rewarded spiritually for the performance of partisan duties. The preacher playing alternately upon both, at once excites an emotional responsiveness that is prepared to obey his slightest injunction; and he does not hesitate to turn this exalted state of feeling to the most useful account. [63]

Today, as in the past, the black churches are a source of political leadership and leaders. For just one example, Rep. William Gray of Pennsylvania, who recently retired as the House Majority Whip, is a practicing minister. The Reverend Jesse Jackson is probably the best-known African American to combine preaching with politicking.

Black churches, for their part, use their political clout to garner support from government officials (especially at the local level). Elected officials, in turn, are quick to reverse the favor by calling on the churches for campaign contributions, volunteers, and votes. This relationship further increases the political leverage of black church leaders. The clergy's strong political role also rests on its professional and economic autonomy. Being obligated to no one outside the black community, they can speak more freely than many other black professionals on controversial issues.

Finally, black churches often combine resources for philanthropic ends, crossing denominational lines to establish, for example, food programs and other basic relief services. These ecumenical programs often go well beyond the basics to encompass complex programs promoting the overall economic welfare of the community. At the national level this collaborative approach is exemplified by the Congress of National Black Churches (CNBC). Founded in 1978, it consists of the seven largest historically black denominations and represents more than 15 million people in some 60,000 churches. Among its other efforts, the CNBC is trying to use its own financial resources to promote black economic development by encouraging the banks it does business with to hire more black employees and make more loans to blacks.

Social and Fraternal Organizations

The most influential black fraternal and social organizations today—the older fraternal orders, and the more recent college fraternities and sororities—are the natural descendants of the benevolent societies formed in the late 18th and early 19th centuries. Although they are primarily social organizations, they continue to regard community service as a major goal, and routinely contribute money and volunteers for charitable purposes.

Many of the earliest fraternal and mutual aid societies are still active, such as African Lodge No. 459, founded around 1787 by Prince Hall. Known today as the Conference of Prince Hall Grand Masters, it has over 5,000 lodges with more than 250,000 members in the U.S., Canada, the Bahamas, and Liberia. These Prince Hall lodges contribute annually to black philanthropic organizations such as the NAACP, the United Negro College Fund, and others. A related fraternal order, founded in 1847 and with 50,000 members today, operates under the lengthy name of The Most Worshipful National Grand Lodge Free and Accepted Ancient York Masons Prince Hall Origin, National Compact, U.S.A., Inc.

Other black fraternal orders that emerged close to the turn of this century have also adapted to modern needs. One such organization, the Ancient Egyptian Arabic Order Nobles Mystic Shrine, Inc., was founded in 1893. With 47,000 members today, this organization runs programs to address delinquency and drug abuse, and supports medical research on health problems of special concern to blacks. Another, the Improved Benevolent Protective Order of Elks of the World, was founded in 1898, and today claims 450,000 members. It supports a variety of causes, including scholarships for which it raises $1 million annually.

Despite such activities, however, many fraternal orders are experiencing dramatic declines in membership, as successful blacks join the growing ranks of collegiate associations instead. The eight largest black fraternities and sororities now have a combined membership of well over 650,000.

The charters of most such organizations stress community

service through charitable giving and volunteering—harking back to W.E.B. Du Bois's charge to the "talented tenth" of educated blacks. Today, virtually all black collegiate fraternities and sororities make annual contributions to black educational charities (e.g.the United Negro College Fund), civil rights organizations, and social welfare endeavors. They also provide volunteers for numerous community activities, with special emphasis on "big brother" and "big sister" programs.

To further strengthen their charitable activities, black sororities have also begun to create separate tax-exempt organizations. For example, the Delta Sigma Theta sorority in Washington, D.C., has established three such institutions: the D.C. Delta Alumnae Foundation, used principally to raise monies for college scholarships; the Delta Housing Corporation, which operates a 500-unit housing facility for the elderly and handicapped; and the D.C. Delta Life Development Corporation, to assist blacks with job training.

The projects carried forward and issues addressed by today's black women through their sororities are, in many respects, the same issues that their great-grandmothers organized to address through the Black Women's Club Movement a century ago: education, employment, housing, and the general well-being and advancement of their community.

New Directions: Black Fundraising Federations

Throughout the country, black organizations provide a wide spectrum of charitable services that communities increasingly depend upon. Heirs to the tradition of mutual aid societies founded two centuries ago principally to help widows and orphans, these institutions provide a wide array of services ranging from voter registration to family counseling, legal aid, and medical services. Like their predecessor organizations, they rely extensively on volunteers, and many such organizations operate as part of a complex network with links to government agencies, churches, and one another.

Finding stable funding for charitable organizations of all types places ever greater demands on staff time and re-

---

The high-stakes race for scarcer dollars has given rise to a new development in black philanthropy: black fund-raising federations.

---

sources. This challenge is perhaps greatest for community-based educational and service organizations. Unlike churches or fraternal organizations, they have no membership to draw on and with very low-income constituencies of their own, they are forced to rely heavily on government funding and private donations to keep their services flowing to their needy constituents. Fund-raising prospects are also affected by relationships with the local United Way, and by the demands that national organizations like the NAACP and the Urban League may place on their local branches.

The increased funding of essential programs by government agencies is, overall, a highly positive development; nevertheless government funding brings with it a unique set of problems. For one thing, lengthy delays in government reimbursement for services often force low-budget agencies to maintain a large cushion of working capital in order to stay afloat between payments. For another, "activist" organizations are often denied municipal grants because they advocate policies that may be unpopular with city officials. During the more penurious '80s, of course, public funding for all social programs became tighter. All in all, it is remarkable how successful many black organizations have been in continuing to offer their services, even in the face of reduced government support.

The high-stakes race for scarcer dollars has given rise to a new development in black philanthropy: black fund-raising federations. These federations represent an innovative solution to the new challenges faced by institutions that serve blacks. These innovations are, in turn, adding new institutional structures to the philanthropic network and, at the same time, opening up a new avenue for black philanthropy.

Prior to the 1960s, black philanthropy could well have been described as "philanthropy among friends." For the most part, the philanthropic efforts of churches, mutual aid societies, and collegiate organizations had focused on aiding individuals within their immediate community. Most of the recipients of this aid were either members of these organizations, or else friends, relatives and others known to members. After the 1960s, however, blacks gradually developed more institutional mechanisms for charitable giving, "philantropy among strangers," including black foundations and private philanthropy by wealthy blacks. Both of these developments are subjects about which only incomplete, anecdotal information currently exists. While these topics lie beyond the scope of this essay, they clearly merit study in their own right.

A third development, the creation of black-oriented federated fund-raising organizations, has particular relevance to this study. The growth of these federations has opened up new opportunities for individual giving by many more non-wealthy blacks, and for giving that reaches beyond the immediate community through these new institutions; as such, it represents a new advancement in black philanthropy. As with past developments in black philanthropy, this new focus is a direct reflection of changing needs and circumstances within the black community.

One likely cause of this shift from community to institutional giving was the dispersal of the black population, particularly in urban areas, that occurred with the decline in housing segregation. Another was the example of the United Funds and Community Chests of the time—federations of nonprofit agencies that raised money collectively, and allocated it to affiliated agencies according to need.

But perhaps the strongest impetus for the formation of these federations was the perceived inequities in allocation of funds by the established federations. As part of their effort to strengthen programs devoted primarily to meeting black

---

The growth of these federations has opened up new opportunities for individual giving by many more non-wealthy blacks, and for giving that reaches beyond the immediate community.

---

needs, black charitable organizations began to form their own fund-raising federations. They acted in the belief that newer organizations representing minority groups and non-traditional interests or causes all too often were denied entry to the United Way system altogether, or else received too small a share of the funds collected.[64]

Once the black federations were established, the next step was to gain access to workplace giving plans run by federal, state and local governments, as well as private employers. Such plans enable employees, through payroll deductions, to make automatic charitable contributions that, when multiplied over the course of a year, amount to far more than most organizations are able to solicit through one-time-only mail campaigns, telephone appeals, or door-to-door canvassing.

The United Black Fund (UBF) of Washington, D.C., a federation of black charities that operates like the United Way, was founded in 1969 by Calvin W. Rolark. The UBF concept took hold after a study revealed that black charities across the country were either being denied funds or were receiving a smaller proportion of the funding pie from their local community chests.[65]

In 1973, the UBF became the first black charitable federation included in Washington's Combined Federal Campaign, an annual fund-raising drive held at federal government worksites. The UBF did so by agreeing to work in partnership with the organization that soon became the United Way of the National Capital Area. The agreement entitles the UBF to all funds from the annual campaign designated directly to it by federal employees, together with 12.5 percent of all funds raised above $14 million.[66]

In addition, the UBF and the United Way of the National Capital Area jointly hold an annual payroll-deduction campaign with the area's private employers. In 1985-86, through the combined receipts from these federal and private campaigns, the UBF was able to distribute $1.68 million to 65 member and 98 nonmember charitable groups. In 1990, UBF distributed over $2.6 million to member and nonmember agencies.

In 1977, the United Black Fund of America was founded to facilitate the formation of local United Black Funds throughout the country, all with the purpose of ensuring that local black charities receive a fair share of their communities' charitable donations. To date, 68 chapters and affiliates of the United Black Fund of America have been established.

The National Black United Fund (NBUF), founded in 1974 by Walter Bremond and currently listing 15 member organizations, is another organization that has attempted to alter or compensate for the priorities of traditional fund-raising organizations. Unlike the United Black Fund, however, whose philosophy is to develop partnerships with United Way, the NBUF defines itself as a black alternative to United Way.[67] NBUF and its affiliates raised over $7 million in 1990.

In 1980 the NBUF won a four-year court battle to allow non-United Way federations to participate in the Combined Federal Campaign.[68] This victory opened up the federal campaign not only to the NBUF, but to a wide range of other non-United Way charities, giving birth to what is known as the Alternative Fund Movement.

The implications for charities participating in workplace giving are dramatic. In 1985, for example, $67 million was pledged to non-United Way charities, more than half of the $130 million total raised by the Combined Federal Campaign in that year.[69] Between 1981 and 1990, after the Federal Campaign was opened to non-United Way charities, the campaign grew from $100 million to $190.4 million. United Way's share of the campaign decreased during the same period from 48.4 percent to 27.7 percent.[70]

The number of states that allow non-United Way charities to participate in their workplace campaigns increased from eight in 1980 to 32 in 1987.[71] However, the local affiliates of NBUF have found it significantly more difficult to gain entree to corporate payroll giving campaigns, particularly at companies where United Way already has been given access.[72] In 1990, United Way raised $3.11 billion, in part from over one million companies and private organizations where it maintains its monopoly position. [73]

In addition to these two national black federations, several local groups have formed independently. For example, Associated Black Charities (ABC) was established in 1982 to serve the black community in New York City. At present, ABC consists of 68 member agencies and has awarded over $3.5 million in grants since its founding.

The strongest reason for black women to organize separately, according to Ruffin, was to refute the negative images of black women then being advanced by many in the women's suffrage movement, which at the time often refused to admit black women as members. These white suffragists were afraid of losing white financial support if they allowed black

---

The strongest reason for black women to organize separately was to refute the negative images of black women then being advanced by many in the women's suffrage movement. . .

---

women to participate.[36] Ruffin also emphasized the special concern of black women for the future of their children—a principal reason black women have been so active in black philanthropy throughout history.

By 1896, black women had launched the National Association of Colored Women, dedicated to social welfare activities. Its motto was "Lifting as We Climb." During this period, various chapters of the organization aided the homeless and maintained employment services, day care centers, and kindergartens. Black women's clubs were, on the whole, a powerful force in charity directed toward the black community.

* * *

A noteworthy aspect of black charitable institutions since the beginning has been their comprehensive nature. Almost all black organizations had to serve a multiplicity of purposes in the earliest days, in response to the conditions of black life. For example, black churches have always provided spiritual, moral, and political leadership, as well as services for the poor. By the same token, black social and fraternal organi-

Conclusion

Ever since the late 1700s black Americans have been pulling together their resources to provide for the neediest among them. Organized charitable giving and volunteering by black Americans can be traced to the earliest black churches, mutual aid societies, and fraternal organizations. These philanthropic institutions, which began by providing the sick and needy with food, clothing and shelter, have developed a complex network of vital services not only within their communities but also to address the needs of the larger black community nationwide.

In addition, black philanthropic efforts (with white support, as well) provided money and people to the black advocacy organizations that have spearheaded major social and political reforms—from the days of the Underground Railroad, to the civil rights movement of the 1960s, to today's workplace giving campaigns.

If this historical picture exposes as unfounded myth the current notion that blacks have no tradition of philanthropy or self-help, it also sheds light on how this myth arose in the first place. The main factors contributing to this

49

misconception are the secrecy under which black organizations were initially forced to work; the focus on meeting needs internal to the black community itself, independent of white institutions or even white awareness; racial stereotyping and segregation; and, more recently, the growth of interracial giving.[74]

The reality differs sharply from the myth: The black community of today draws on a strong tradition of people helping others to help themselves. In recent years, there has been an increase in multiracial philanthropy, with donors of both races actively supporting "colorblind" efforts to serve the needy of all backgrounds. Nevertheless, the number and variety of on-going charitable activities under black auspices continue to constitute an extensive, thriving black philanthropy that can be distinguished from the charitable efforts of the larger society, even today.

As research conducted under the auspices of the Joint Center for Political and Economic Study has shown, black philanthropy and self-help are alive and well. Despite the fact that their income levels are lower than those of whites, black Americans are as likely as whites to make charitable contributions, and the size of contributions are essentially the same.

Black philanthropy is a rich tapestry that is still being woven today. With its crossthreads formed over two centuries of tradition and creative responses to emerging needs, black philanthropy reflects a longstanding commitment by black Americans to improving the lives of their brothers, sisters, and selves. Black philanthropy today, as in the past, is dedicated to fostering and preserving the values of compassion, self-help, and hard work that are the foundation of the black community.

Notes

1   Committee on Policy for Racial Justice, Joint Center for Political Studies, *Black Initiative and Governmental Responsibility.*

2   Readers may wonder why this historical summary focuses on organizations rather than individuals. There are two reasons. First, there is very little historical information about the philanthropic activities of individual blacks. Although wealthy black philanthropists did exist in the early period—for example, Paul Cuffee, who lived in Massachusetts in the 1790s—they were rare. Second, and even more important, early charitable giving and voluntarism in black communities occurred most often through local black organizations such as churches, a practice necessitated by the extremely limited resources of black freedmen.

The facts summarized in this extended essay are drawn from diverse sources scattered throughtout the historical literature, but four authorities deserve special credit for the value derived from their books: Benjamin Quarles' *The Negro in the Making of America* (1979); Abram Harris's *The Negro as Capitalist* (1968); E. Franklin Frazier's *The Negro Church in America* (1974); and August Meier's *Negro Thought in America: 1880-1915* (1983).

3   See C. Eric Lincoln and Lawrence H. Mamiya, *The Black Church in the African American Experience.*

4   Filer Commission on Private Philanthropy and *Public Needs, Giving in America: Toward a Stronger Voluntary Sector*, p. 37.

5   David Mathews, "The Independent Sector and the Political Responsibilities of the Public," p. 6.

6   E. Franklin Frazier, *The Negro Church in America*, p. 41.

7   Lawrence N. Jones, "The Early Black Societies and Churches: Matrix of Community and Mission, 1778-1830," p. 2.

8   Concerning the founding of Allen's and Jones' churches, see Frazier, 1974, p. 33. The creation of the A.M.E. denomination is covered in Quarles, 1979, p. 100. The Free African Society's statement of mission is quoted in Wilmore, 1983, p. 25.

9   Lawrence N. Jones, "Serving the Least of These," p. 5.

10   Concerning the Free African Society's finances, see A. Harris, 1968, p. 21; concerning the group's humanitarian aid during Philadelphia's plague of 1793, see Quarles, 1979, p. 98;

and for its abolitionist activity, see Bennett et al., 1971, p. 198.

11   The founding and activities of Boston's Sons of the African Society are discussed in Wilmore, 1983, p. 98; concerning the society's 1808 commemoration, see Horton and Horton, 1979, p. 28.

12   Robert L. Harris, "Early Black Benevolent Societies, 1780-1830," pp. 608-609.

13   Lerone Bennett, Jr., et al., editors, *Pictorial History of Black America*, vol. 1, p. 183.

14   R. Harris, "Early Black Benevolent Societies, 1780-1830," pp. 613-614.

15   August Meier, *Negro Thought in America*, 1880-1915, p. 14.

16   King E. Davis, *Fund Raising in the Black Community: History, Feasibility, and Conflict*, p. 4.

17   A. Harris, 1968, pp. 20-21. While it is not possible to accurately convert these mid-nineteenth-century dollars into today's currency, the sums cited here are clearly sizable for their time.

18   R. Harris, "Early Black Benevolent Societies, 1780-1830," p. 606.

19   James A. Joseph, "Black Philanthropy: The Potential and Limits of Private Generosity in a Civil Society."

20   Concerning the Brown Fellowship Society, see Frazier, 1974, p. 44. The New York African Society is discussed in R. Harris, 1979, p. 615.

21   Boston's and Philadelphia's black literary societies are discussed in Quarles, 1979, p. 98.

22   For the beginnings of the Underground Railroad, see Bennett, et al., 1971, p. 226. The contribution of black businessmen is discussed in Walker, 1986, p. 376.

23   Larry Gara, "William Still and the Underground Railroad," pp. 344-345.

24   Frazier, *The Negro Church in America*, p. 42.

25   For more on the Hayes-Tilden compromise, see Bennett, 1982, pp. 235-254.

26   Meier, *Negro Thought in America 1880-1915*, p. 121.

27   A. Harris, *The Negro as Capitalist*, p. 47.

28   Concerning the Grand Order of the Odd Fellows' founding, see Quarles, 1979, p. 97. Concerning the group's growth, see Meier, 1983, p. 137. The antislavery activity of the Order of the Twelve Knights and the Daughters of Tabor is covered in Meier, 1983, p. 15.

29   A. Harris, *The Negro as Capitalist*, p. 47.

30   For the A.M.E. church's funding of colleges and universities, see Jones, 1984. For the work of the Baptist Home Missionary Society, see Meier, 1983, pp. 132-133. Concerning the schools built by Julius Rosenwald, see Frazier, 1974, p. 46.

31   Darlene Clark Hine, "Communal Agency and Self-Reclamation: The Philanthropic Work of Black Women," in *Women and Philanthropy: Past, Present and Future.*

32   James Oliver Horton and Lois E. Horton, *Black Bostonians*, pp. 31-32.

33   The Daughters of Tabor is discussed in Meier, 1983, p. 15; the White Rose Industrial Association in Meier, 1983, p. 134. Concerning the beneficiaries of these organizations, see M.W. Davis, 1982, p. 90.

34   For more on the black women's club movement, see Giddings, 1984.

35   Charles H. Wesley, *The History of the National Association of Colored Women's Clubs: A Legacy of Service*, pp. 33-34.

36   This is in no way meant to belittle the earlier efforts of white women, such as Sarah and Angelina Grimke, who began to speak out against slavery and, subsequently, to advocate women's rights beginning in the 1830s. For a fuller account see Evans, 1979, pp. 25-27.

37   The Farmer's Improvement Society and the Afro-American League are both discussed in Meier 1983, pp. 123-124 and 128-129, respectively.

38   Quoted in Broderick and Meier, 1965, pp. 58-59.

39   *Ibid.*, p. 60.

40   Charles H. Wesley, *Henry Arthur Callis: Life and Legacy,* p. 279.

41   Paula Giddings has written an entire book about this sorority and its influence: *In Search of Sisterhood: Delta Sigma Theta and the Challenge of the Black Sorority Movement* (1988).

42   Lerone Bennett, Jr., *A History of Black America*, p. 194.

43   Benjamin Quarles, *The Negro in the Making of America*, p. 198.

44   *Ibid.*, p. 175.

45   The violence of this period is evident in the extraordinary number of documented lynchings. At least 64 blacks were murdered this way in 1918, while in 1919, 83 blacks were lynched and 11 burned alive. See Bennett et al., 1971, p. 294.

46   Bennett et al., *Pictorial History of Black America*, p. 198.

47   Francis L. Broderick and August Meier, *Negro Protest Thought in the Twentieth Century*, p. 60.

48   Meier, *Negro Thought in America 1880-1915*, p. 132.

49   For details on the role of white philanthropists in funding black educational endeavors, see Quarles, 1979, p. 165; and Meier, 1983, p. 132. An interesting discussion of the issue by Booker T. Washington, from his article, "Raising Money," is reprinted in O'Connell, 1983.

50   Davis, *Fund Raising in the Black Community*, pp. 10-11.

51   Robert A. Hill, "The First England Years and After, 1912-1916," p. 60.

52   John Henrik Clarke, ed., *Marcus Garvey and the Vision of Africa*, p. 199.

53   Richard B. Moore, "The Critics and Opponents of Marcus Garvey," p. 228.

54   From Garvey's article, "Why the Black Star Line Failed," quoted in Clarke, 1973, p. 141.

55   Quarles, *The Negro in the Making of America*, p. 209.

56   Father Divine is discussed in Weisbrot, 1984, and in Bennett et al., 1971, p. 215.

57   Bennett, *A History of Black America*, p. 306.

58   Broderick and Meier, *Negro Protest Thought in the Twentieth Century*, pp. 204-205.

59   *Ibid.*, p. 241.

60   James M. Washington, *A Testament of Hope: The Essential Writings and Speeches of Martin Luther King, Jr.*, pp. 217-223.

61   The Nation of Islam's founding is described in Lincoln, 1969, p. 10; its rehabilitation efforts are discussed in the same (p. 24).

62   Emmett D. Carson, "Patterns of Giving in Black Churches," in *Faith and Philanthropy in America*, pp. 232-252.

63   This excerpt from Philip A. Bruce's *The Plantation Negro as a Freeman* (published in 1889 by Putnam) is quoted in Wilmore, 1983, pp. 75-76.

64   Emmett D. Carson, "The Attitudes, Accessibility, and Participation of Blacks and Whites in Work-Site Charitable Payroll Deduction Plans."

65   National Black Monitor, "The United Black Fund: A Vital New Vehicle for Blacks To Begin Leading Blacks," p. 7.

66   *Ibid.*, p. 12.

67   For more on the philosophy behind the National Black United Fund, see Bremond, 1976, and Blakewell, 1976.

68   NCRP, *Charity Begins at Work*, 1986, p. 25.

69   NCRP, "The Workplace Giving Revolution: A Special Report," p. 1.

70   Bruce Millar, "United Way Rivals Gain Ground."

71   NCRP, "The Workplace Giving Revolution," p. 1.

72   See Polivy, 1985, and National Committee for Responsive Philanthropy, 1986.

73   See Bruce Millar, "United Way Rivals Gain Ground," p. 1.

74   Emmett D. Carson, "Contemporary Trends in Black Philanthropy: Challenging the Myths," pp. 219-238.

Works Cited

Bennett, Lerone Jr. 1969. *A History of Black America.* Chicago: Johnson Publishing Company.

——————. 1982. *Before the Mayflower: A History of Black America.* New York: Penguin Books.

Bennett, Lerone Jr., et al., editors. 1971. *Pictorial History of Black America*, vol. 1. Nashville, Tenn.: Ebony and The Southwestern Company.

Blakewell, Danny J.X. 1976. "The Brotherhood Crusade: A Conceptual Model." *The Black Scholar*, vol. 7, no. 6 (March 1976): 22-26.

Bremond, Walter. 1976. "The National Black United Fund Movement." *The Black Scholar*, vol. 7, no. 6 (March 1976): 10-15.

Broderick, Francis L., and August Meier. 1965. *Negro Protest Thought in the Twentieth Century.* New York: Bobbs-Merrill Company.

Carson, Emmett D. 1988. "The Attitudes, Accessibility, and Participation of Blacks and Whites in Work-Site Charitable Payroll Deduction Plans." Working paper. Center for The Study of Philanthropy and Voluntarism, Duke University.

—————————. 1989. *The Charitable Appeals Fact Book*. Washington, D.C.: Joint Center for Political Studies Press.

—————————. 1990. "Patterns of Giving in Black Churches." In *Faith and Philanthropy in America* (San Francisco: Jossey-Bass Publishers).

—————————. 1991. "Contemporary Trends in Black Philanthropy: Challenging the Myths." In *Taking Fund Raising Seriously*, edited by Dwight F. Burlingame and Lamont J. Halse. San Francisco: Jossey-Bass Publishers.

Clarke, John Henrik, ed. 1973. *Marcus Garvey and the Vision of Africa*. New York: Vintage Books.

Committee on Policy for Racial Justice. 1987. *Black Initiative and Governmental Responsibility*. Washington, D.C.: Joint Center for Political Studies.

Davis, King E. 1975. *Fund Raising in the Black Community: History, Feasibility, and Conflict*. Metuchen, N.J.: The Scarecrow Press.

Davis, Marianna W. 1982. *Contributions of Black Women*. Columbia, S.C.: Kenday Press.

Evans, Sara. 1979. *Personal Politics: The Roots of Women's*

Liberation in the Civil Rights Movement and the New Left. New York: Alfred A. Knopf.

Filer Commission on Private Philanthropy and Public Needs. 1975. *Giving in America: Toward a Stronger Voluntary Sector.* (Place of publication not available.)

Frazier, E. Franklin. 1974. *The Negro Church in America.* New York: Schocken Books.

Gara, Larry. 1972. "William Still and the Underground Railroad." In *Blacks in White America Before 1865,* edited by Robert V. Haynes. New York: David McKay Company.

Giddings, Paula. 1984. *When and Where I Enter.* New York: William Morrow and Company.

——————. 1988. *In Search of Sisterhood: Delta Sigma Theta and the Challenge of the Black Sorority Movement.* New York: William Morrow and Company.

Harris, Abram. 1968. *The Negro as Capitalist.* College Park, Md.: McGrath Publishing Company.

Harris, Robert L. 1979. "Early Black Benevolent Societies, 1780-1830." *The Massachusetts Review* 20 (Autumn 1979): 608-609.

Hill, Robert A. 1973. "The First England Years and After, 1912-1916." In *Marcus Garvey and the Vision of Africa* (see Clarke, 1973).

Hine, Darlene Clark. 1987. "Communal Agency and Self-

Reclamation: The Philanthropic Work of Black Women."
In *Women and Philanthropy: Past, Present and Future*. New
York: Center for the Study of Philanthropy (City Univer-
sity of New York).

Horton, James Oliver, and Lois E. Horton. 1979. *Black
Bostonians*. New York: Holmes and Meier, Publishers.

Jones, Lawrence N. 1977. "The Early Black Societies and
Churches: Matrix of Community and Mission, 1778-1830."
In *The Black Church: A Community Resource*. Washington,
D.C.: Institute for Urban Affairs and Research (Howard
University).

—————. 1984. "Serving the Least of These." *Foundation News*, vol. 25, no. 5 (September/October 1984): 5.

Joseph, James A. 1991. "Black Philanthropy: The Potential
and Limits of Private Generosity in a Civil Society." First
Annual Lecture delivered to The Association of Black
Foundation Executives, June 3, 1991, Washington, D.C.

Kutscher, Ronald E. 1987. "Overview and Implications of
the Projections to 2000." *Monthly Labor Review*, vol. 110,
no. 9 (September 1987): 3-9.

Landry, Bart. 1987. *The New Black Middle Class*. Berkeley:
University of California Press.

Lincoln, C. Eric. 1969. *The Black Muslims*. Boston: Beacon
Press.

—————. and Lawrence H. Mamiya. 1990. *The Black*

Church in the African American Experience. Durham, N.C.:
Duke University Press.

Mathews, David. 1987. "The Independent Sector and the
Political Responsibilities of the Public." Address made in
New York City on March 19, 1987, before the Spring
Research Forum held by Independent Sector.

McClester, Cedric. 1985. "Black Charity Battles for Share
of Payroll Deductions." *Big Red News,* August 3, 1985: 2.

Meier, August. 1983. *Negro Thought in America 1880-1915.*
Ann Arbor: University of Michigan Press.

Millar, Bruce, 1991. "United Way Rivals Gain Ground."
The Chronicle on Philanthropy, Vol. IV, No. 4 (December 3,
1991).

Moore, Richard B. 1973. "The Critics and Opponents of
Marcus Garvey." In *Marcus Garvey and the Vision of Africa*
(see Clarke, 1973).

National Black Monitor. 1984. "The United Black Fund: A
Vital New Vehicle for Blacks To Begin Leading Blacks."
National Black Monitor 9 (September 1984).

NCRP (National Committee for Responsive Philanthropy).
1986. *Charity Begins at Work.* Washington, D.C.

——————. 1987b. "The Workplace Giving Revolution:
A Special Report." Washington, D.C.

O'Connell, Brian, ed. 1983. *America's Voluntary Spirit: A*

Book of Readings. Washington, D.C.: Independent Sector.

—————————. 1987a. *Philanthropy in Action.* Washington, D.C.: The Foundation Center.

—————————. 1987b. *State of the Sector: With Particular Attention to Its Independence.* Washington, DC: Independent Sector.

Polivy, Deborah K. 1985. "Increasing Giving Options in Corporate Charitable Payroll Deduction Programs: Who Benefits?" Working paper. Program on Nonprofit Organizations, Yale University.

Quarles, Benjamin. 1979. *The Negro in the Making of America.* New York: Collier Books.

—————————. [1986]. *Household Wealth and Asset Ownership: 1984* (Household Economic studies, Series P-70, no. 7, July 1986). Washington, D.C.: U.S. Government Printing Office.

United Way of America. 1985. "What Lies Ahead—A Mid-Decade View." Alexandria, Va.: United Way of America.

Walker, Juliet E. K. 1986. "Racism, Slavery, and Free Enterprise: Black Entrepreneurship in the United States before the Civil War." *Business History Review*, Autumn 1986.

Washington, James M. 1986. *A Testament of Hope: The*

Essential Writings and Speeches of Martin Luther King, Jr. San Francisco: Harper San Francisco.

Wesley, Charles H. 1977. *Henry Arthur Callis: Life and Legacy.* Chicago: The Foundation Publishers.

—————. 1984. *The History of the National Association of Colored Women's Clubs: A Legacy of Service.* Washington, D.C.: Mercury Press.

Wilmore, Gayraud S. 1983. *Black Religion and Black Radicalism.* New York: Orbis Books.

About the Author

Emmett D. Carson is a program officer in the Governance and Public Policy Program at the Ford Foundation. In that capacity, he is responsible for the Foundation's efforts to promote and strengthen philanthropy and the nonprofit sector in the United States and abroad. He has also worked in the Foundation's Rights and Opportunities Program in the area of minority rights and opportunities. Before joining the Ford Foundation, Dr. Carson directed the first national study of black philanthropy at the Joint Center for Political and Economic Studies.

Dr. Carson is a graduate of Morehouse College and received his master's and Ph.D. degrees from Princeton University. He has written and lectured widely on philanthropy and poverty issues. In addition, he has served on numerous boards and advisory committees, including the Association of Black Foundation Executives, the Council on Foundations, and Independent Sector. Dr. Carson and his wife Lisa currently make their home in New Jersey.

Joint Center Books of Related Interest

THE CHARITABLE APPEALS FACT BOOK
How Blacks and Whites Respond to Different Types of Fundraising Efforts
by Emmett D. Carson (1989)

"KEEP HOPE ALIVE!"
Super Tuesday and Jesse Jackson's 1988 Campaign for the Presidency
by Penn Kimball (1992)

BANKING ON BLACK ENTERPRISE
The Potential of Emerging Firms for Revitalizing Urban Economies
by Timothy Bates (1993)

VOTING RIGHTS IN AMERICA
Continuing the Quest for Full Participation
edited by Karen McGill Arrington and
William L. Taylor (1993)

For ordering information, contact
UNIVERSITY PRESS OF AMERICA
4720 Boston Way
Lanham, Maryland 20706